IDA B. WELLS-BARNETT

Ida B. Wells-Barnett

Powerhouse with a Pen

Catherine A. Welch

**TRAILBLAZER
BIOGRAPHY**

CAROLRHODA BOOKS, INC./MINNEAPOLIS

To Lucy, Marian, and Sharon

My thanks to Ingrid Davis, Cynthia Baklik, Mary Ellen Delaney, and the staff of the Monroe (Connecticut) Public Library for their help in gathering material for this book.

Carolrhoda Books, Inc.,
A Division of Lerner Publishing Group
241 First Avenue North,
Minneapolis, MN 55401 U.S.A.

Website address: www.lernerbooks.com

Library of Congress Cataloging-in-Publication Data

Welch, Catherine A.
   Ida B. Wells-Barnett : powerhouse with a pen / by Catherine A. Welch.
     p.   cm. — (Trailblazers)
   Includes bibliographical references and index.
   Summary: The story of the African American woman who used her talents as a speaker and journalist to work for the civil rights of black people.
     ISBN 1-57505-352-7 (lib. bdg. : alk. paper)
   1. Wells-Barnett, Ida B., 1862–1931—Juvenile literature. 2. Afro-American women civil rights workers—Biography—Juvenile literature.
3. Civil rights workers—United States—Biography—Juvenile literature.
4. Journalists—United States—Biography—Juvenile literature. 5. United States—Race relations—Juvenile literature. [1. Wells-Barnett, Ida B., 1862–1931. 2. Civil rights workers. 3. Afro-Americans—Biography. 4. Race relations. 5. Women—Biography.] I. Title.
E185.97.W55W45 1999
323'.092—dc21   99-35291
[B]

Manufactured in the United States of America
1 2 3 4 5 6 – JR – 05 04 03 02 01 00

CONTENTS

Ida B. Wells was freed from slavery at the age of three, but she spent the rest of her life fighting for equal rights.

1

A STRONG, BRIGHT PRESENCE

Ida B. Wells was born a slave. But she never knew the sting of a whip lashed across her back. She never knew the terror of being dragged from her mother's arms and sold to strangers. Ida was born in Holly Springs, Mississippi, on July 16, 1862, during the Civil War. Before she was three, the war was over, and the nation's four million slaves had been freed.

Ida's life was not controlled by a white plantation owner and his family. Instead of working in scorching sun-baked fields or cooking in a white woman's kitchen, Ida went to school. Instead of having nightmares of a slave in a plantation shack, Ida had hopeful dreams in a house built and owned by her father.

Usually, freed slaves had no jobs, no money, no special skills, and no land. As slaves, they had not been allowed to learn to read. They often ended up working in the fields for their former masters. But Ida's father had carpentry skills, so he had no problem finding work after the war. The Wells family had the chance for a good life.

Ida's parents were bright and independent thinkers. They were not controlled by what other people thought. Ida grew up believing she was worthy of the same rights and privileges as a white person. But while Ida had bright dreams for her future, many white people were working to "keep the Negro down."

The Emancipation Proclamation had freed the slaves, but the Civil War had left many Southern towns in ruins, and many white people angry and bitter. Plantation mansions had been wrecked and burned by Union soldiers from the North. Roads and railroads had been destroyed,

After the Civil War, many Southern towns had to recover from the destruction brought on by battles with Northern soldiers.

and people were left struggling to find food and clothing. Losing the war forced many Southern white families to do something they had never done before. Without unpaid slave labor, they had to do their own work or pay black workers to do it.

After the Civil War, many Southern whites vowed to pass laws that would deny black people justice and fair treatment. Many whites did not believe that blacks were equally people—human beings. They did not want blacks to go to school and learn to read. They did not want black men to vote, own property, or hold public office. Even though whites could no longer own slaves, many still treated blacks as slaves. And while some whites planned to pass unfair laws, other white people were even willing to kill to keep control of blacks.

But Ida was determined not to let white threats keep her down. Ida wanted justice and fair treatment for herself and for her people, and she would not settle for less.

Although most blacks and whites at this time were afraid to see and speak the truth, Ida spent a lifetime daring to find the truth. And when she did, she traveled, gave speeches, wrote for newspapers, and organized groups to work for change. She dared the world to see the truth.

2

A CHILD IN HOLLY SPRINGS

Although Ida did not grow up as a slave, her parents did. Her mother, Elizabeth Warrenton, was born in Virginia and suffered a terrifying life as a slave. Elizabeth was beaten by her white owners. She and two of her sisters were taken from their family in Virginia by slave traders and sold to a white family in Mississippi. Elizabeth lived in constant fear—unsure of what each day would bring. When would she get the next beating? Would she be sold again?

Eventually, Elizabeth Warrenton was sold again. This time, she was bought by a builder named Mr. Bolling, who lived in Holly Springs, Mississippi. There she worked in his house as a cook, where she met Ida's father, James Wells.

Ida's parents met, married, and began to raise their family in Holly Springs, Mississippi.

James Wells was the son of a white plantation owner, Mr. Wells, and a slave woman, Peggy. The plantation was in Tippah County, Mississippi, not far from Holly Springs. Since Mr. Wells's wife, Miss Polly, never had children, James had a special place in the Wells's household. He was never beaten or sold. Mr. Wells wanted James to have carpentry skills to use on the plantation. So, unlike most slaves—who worked in the fields— James was given a chance to learn a trade. When James

A pastor visits a young family of former slaves, much like the young Wells family.

was eighteen, Mr. Wells arranged for him to be an apprentice to Mr. Bolling in Holly Springs.

James never returned to the Wells's plantation. He and Elizabeth married, although as slaves they couldn't marry legally. Then in 1862, in the midst of the Civil War, Elizabeth gave birth to their first child, Ida Bell Wells.

In May 1865, when the war ended in Mississippi and freedom finally came, James and Elizabeth prayed and shouted for joy. Like many former slaves, they celebrated their new freedom by marrying again, this time in a legal wedding ceremony. They rejoiced that their children would never be taken away from them and sold. They looked forward to sending their children to school.

James continued to work in Mr. Bolling's carpentry

shop as a paid employee. As free people, James and Elizabeth were able to come and go as they pleased, traveling on trains for picnics and holidays, planning and making their own decisions about their future. For Ida's father, making his own decisions about the future meant becoming involved in politics. James went to meetings where black men talked about how to gain equal rights with white men. He was interested in knowing about the activities of the state's lawmakers. He wanted to see black men in important positions in government.

In 1867, when black men in Mississippi were allowed to vote for the first time, James joined other former slaves and voted. Like many black men, he voted for the Republican candidate. President Lincoln had been a Republican. Republicans had ended slavery, given black

Black men stand in long lines to register to vote for the first time.

men the right to vote, and supported civil rights for black people. Democrats had been known as the party of slaveholders.

James angered Mr. Bolling by not voting for a Democrat, even though some of the most well-regarded white men in Holly Springs had become Republicans. The day James voted for a Republican, Mr. Bolling locked James out of his shop.

James wasn't concerned. He started his own carpentry business and had no trouble finding work. The war had destroyed many buildings, and James had skills that many white people did not. He bought a set of tools, rented a house, and started a new life for his family.

Holly Springs was a town of rolling hills and rippling rivers. As a young child, Ida attended school. She and Eugenia, Jim, and their little brother, George, went to a school called Shaw University. This school had been founded by a Methodist minister from the North who wanted to help educate Southern blacks. Elizabeth went, too, so she could learn to read the Bible. Ida's father became one of the trustees of the school.

The teachers at the school were white Christians from the North. Ida thought these men and women were intelligent and good examples of Christian courage. Ida read everything she could get her hands on, though she never read anything written by black authors or about black people. All the schoolbooks were written by white authors about white people.

Ida's teachers gave lessons in reading and writing. They also encouraged Ida to work hard, to be disciplined

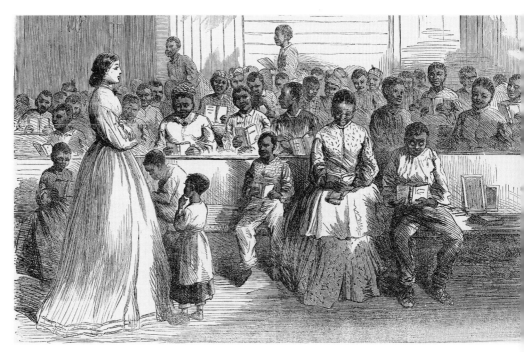

After the Civil War, many black people—both children and adults—attended school for the first time. Ida's mother went to school with her children.

and responsible, and to serve others. The Christian teachers encouraged Ida to act like a lady at all times.

Being ladylike was important to Ida. Former slaves, like her mother, worked particularly hard to be ladylike. As slaves, they had worked long hard hours in the fields. At the end of each day, their backs had ached and their hands had become callused.

After the war, black women looked forward to being treated like white women. They wanted to stay inside the house, take care of their own children, and do the household chores for their own family only. They wanted men to respect them the way they respected white women.

They felt they would get that respect if they looked and acted like ladies. White gloves, fine manners, and starched curtains became important to them.

Ida's mother taught many of the same values at home that Ida was learning at Shaw. She handled Ida and her younger siblings with strict discipline. Each night, the children had to complete their homework and do their chores.

Ida was responsible for the Saturday night chores. She made sure that the family's shoes were shined and clothes were pressed for Sunday's church services. She made sure she and her siblings—Eugenia, Jim, George, and the new baby, Annie—took baths. Each week, their mother took them to Sunday school. Elizabeth had a deep faith in God, and she wanted to raise her children with that faith.

3

ROOTS OF COURAGE

When the old folks talked about slave times, Ida listened. One day Ida overheard a conversation between her father and his mother, Grandma Peggy. Peggy told James that Miss Polly, his father's wife, wanted to see him and the children. Ida heard her father reply with angry words. Miss Polly had ordered his mother to be stripped and whipped the day his father died, and James had never forgotten it. James hated Miss Polly and never wanted to see her again.

Ida hung onto every word her father spoke. She was scared, but she wanted to know more. Her father seemed angry that Grandma Peggy had forgiven Miss Polly. Ida heard her father say that Grandma Peggy had saved Polly from starving to death.

What did her father mean? wondered Ida. She wanted to ask questions. She wanted to know the truth. But she didn't dare ask her father or grandmother. She knew they would be angry if she interfered with their adult conversation.

Ida also listened when her mother told stories about her life as a slave. It was difficult for Ida to listen to the stories and to picture her mother being beaten.

As a child, Ida learned about the slow progress blacks were making toward equal rights. Proud that Ida could read, her father encouraged Ida to read the newspaper to him. This was the time of Reconstruction following the Civil War—a time of changes and rebuilding in the South. Ida listened to her father and his friends discuss the political events of the day. Some of the news gave them hope. In some areas, black voters outnumbered white voters. Some black men, including friends of Ida's father, were elected to public office. And at that time in Holly Springs, white and black politicians, Democrats and Republicans, got along with each other.

But while Ida heard these words of encouragement, she heard other words as well. She heard about the Ku Klux Klan, or KKK. The KKK wanted to make sure white people held onto their power in the South. So members of this secret society terrorized blacks and the whites who supported them.

When Ida was young, she did not know exactly what the KKK was. But she knew it was something to fear. The KKK looked for ways to frighten black men from being active in politics. Ida knew that her father went to political meetings at night. She knew these meetings were dangerous for everyone there. She watched her mother pace the floor until her father returned.

Ida's mother had good reason to be worried at night when her husband was gone. It was during the night

Members of the Ku Klux Klan in disguise in the 1870s

when the KKK, their faces hidden under hoods, rode throughout the countryside. They set houses on fire. They dragged both black and white people from their homes. They whipped and murdered people. No one was safe.

Ida's family never had to face the terror of KKK violence. And the KKK probably didn't kill any black people in the county where Ida lived. But black people there always lived in fear of the KKK. Despite this, Ida's parents were brave. Her father continued his political activity. And through their example, Ida's parents gave their daughter roots of courage.

For most of her childhood, Ida's life in Holly Springs was a peaceful one. By 1878, when Ida was sixteen, she had six younger brothers and sisters—Eugenia, Jim, George, Annie, Lily, and Stanley. One brother, Eddie, had died. Ida and her family often visited Grandma Peggy at her farm in Tippah County or their Aunt Fannie in Memphis, Tennessee.

But in 1878, yellow fever broke out in New Orleans, Louisiana. At that time, there was no treatment or cure for yellow fever. It was spread by the bite of a mosquito, but people thought it was passed from person to person.

Ida was visiting Grandma Peggy when she learned the disease had spread to Memphis. Soon after, Holly Springs was hit, and Ida received a letter from home telling her that her mother and father had died of yellow fever.

Ida was grief stricken and wanted to rush home to her younger brothers and sisters. At first her grandmother persuaded Ida not to go. She was afraid Ida would get sick and die, too. But three days later, Ida received a letter from a doctor in Holly Springs urging her to return. Ida persuaded her grandmother to let her go, and she headed for Holly Springs by train.

When the train stopped at a town along the way, the people at the station were horrified to hear that Ida was headed for Holly Springs. She would get sick, they warned her. She would die. Then who would take care of her brothers and sisters? They pleaded with Ida to wait until the yellow fever was no longer a threat.

At first, Ida listened to their advice and changed her mind about going to Holly Springs. But she kept thinking about her younger brothers and sisters. She thought about how much they were suffering and how scared they must be now that their parents were dead. She just had to go and be with them.

Ida took a freight train for the rest of the trip home, since no passenger train would dare go to Holly Springs. Again, she was warned to turn back. The conductor of the train was sure Ida would get sick and die. But Ida felt it was her duty to go home—and that's exactly what she did.

Yellow fever had hit Holly Springs hard. Over half the population had left town, and most of the people who

When yellow fever hit the South in 1878, many lost their lives. Ida's father, a carpenter, built coffins and dug graves for those who had died.

stayed became sick. When Ida got to town, she found the streets deserted. She got home to find two of the children sick. The baby, Stanley, had already died.

Though still just a teenager, Ida took charge of family matters. She met Dr. Gray, a white man who had helped the Wells family. After James and Elizabeth had died, Dr. Gray had made sure that the Wells children were not left alone, but cared for by the Howard Association. He had

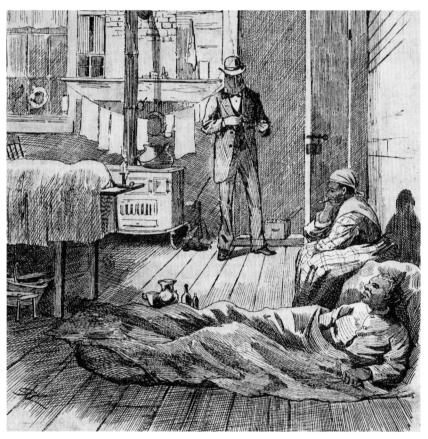

A doctor makes his rounds during the yellow fever outbreak. Dr. Gray, a white man, had known Ida's father, and he helped the Wells children after their parents died.

put the family's savings of three hundred dollars in a downtown safe. He spoke with admiration of James Wells. He told Ida how her father had remained cheerful in spite of the fear that gripped the town. James had done what he could to help others. He had prayed with the dying and built coffins for the dead.

Ida was touched by Dr. Gray's concern and kindness. In this time of suffering, Ida took comfort in knowing that a white person cared enough about her family to help.

In the autumn, after the yellow fever outbreak was over, friends of the family met in the Wells parlor to discuss what should be done with the children. No one thought to ask Ida what she thought was best. Two women offered to take five-year-old Annie and two-year-old Lily. Two men offered homes and a chance to learn carpentry to eleven-year-old Jim and nine-year-old George.

But no one wanted Eugenia, who had been paralyzed from the waist down two years earlier. The family friends wanted to put her in a poorhouse—and they decided that Ida was old enough to take care of herself.

Ida believed she could take care of more than herself. And she knew her parents would have been heartbroken to think that their children were scattered among different homes. Her father had left them a house and some money. Ida decided that she would find a job and take care of all the children.

Ida knew it would be difficult. This decision meant the end of her carefree childhood. It meant it would be hard to continue her schooling. But Ida knew she had to keep the family together.

A large group of black children play outside of their school in the rural South.

During the week, Ida taught the children of poor, black farmers to read and write. At the beginning of each week, she rode her mule to a one-room country school-house six miles outside of town. She earned twenty-five dollars a month. Her students' parents also paid her with eggs and butter. Grandma Peggy moved to Holly Springs to help care for Ida's sisters and brothers. On Fridays, Ida rode her mule back to town and spent her weekends cooking, washing clothes, and ironing.

When Grandma Peggy had a stroke, she had to move back to her farm. A friend of Elizabeth's took over and helped Ida with the children during the week.

Ida kept up her exhausting schedule for over two years. When she was nineteen, two of her aunts offered to help with the children. Eugenia and the boys moved to Aunt Belle's farm. Annie and Lily went to Memphis to live with their Aunt Fannie, their father's sister, who was a widow with three children. Ida also went to Memphis and lived with Aunt Fannie.

It was sad to see the family break up. But Ida realized she would have the freedom to make a life for herself.

4

POWERHOUSE WITH A PEN

Nineteen-year-old Ida was bright, restless, and full of energy. Memphis offered many opportunities. It was a city of cobblestone streets, hundreds of factories, ten railroads, a sewer system, theaters, waterfront steamboats, and cotton barges. Thousands of freed slaves had flocked to the city after the Civil War.

By the time Ida reached Memphis, black people had built churches and schools. The city offered many cultural and educational opportunities for blacks as well as whites. Black people could ride on the same streetcars as whites. Black men could vote and serve in public office.

The first black senator *(far left)* and representatives from Mississippi, South Carolina, Alabama, Georgia, and Florida were part of the U.S. Congress in 1872.

Ida wrote about her new life in her diary. She got a job teaching in a country school in Woodstock, outside of Memphis. And she began to study for the exam to teach in the Memphis city schools. As in Holly Springs, she traveled to the country—this time by train—and taught during the week. In the evenings, she read by firelight — the Bible, novels by Charles Dickens and Louisa May Alcott, and plays by William Shakespeare. On weekends, she took the train back into Memphis to stay with her Aunt Fannie.

In May 1884, Ida caught her usual train from Memphis to Woodstock. After choosing a seat, as usual, in the ladies' car—the first-class car—she handed the conductor her ticket. But on this particular day, the conductor refused to take the ticket and told Ida she had to move to the forward car—the one for smokers and blacks. The laws had changed, and black people no longer had the same legal rights as whites. But Ida refused to move. She had paid for a first-class ticket, and she was a lady. She remained in her seat and kept reading the book in her hands.

The conductor became angry and grabbed her. He tried to pull Ida out of her seat. But as soon as he touched her, Ida bit his hand. Then she thrust her feet straight out into the seat in front of her.

A conductor tries to expel a black man from a railway car reserved for white people. The same thing happened to Ida on her usual route from Memphis to Woodstock.

At that point, the conductor stormed off. While he was getting help, some of the white ladies and their gentlemen friends stood on their seats to see what was happening.

Minutes later Ida heard the crowd cheer and clap as three men approached and yanked her out of the seat, ripping the sleeves of her linen coat. When the train stopped at the next station, Ida got off. She refused to go into the smoking car.

Ida was shaken by the experience and determined to right this wrong. When she returned to Memphis the next weekend, she hired a lawyer—the only black lawyer she knew in Memphis. She asked him to sue the railroad.

By the fall of 1884, Ida had passed the Memphis teachers' exam. While she was waiting for the case to go to court, Ida got a job teaching first grade in the Memphis city schools. But she was not happy as a teacher. In her diary, Ida wrote about her experiences with her large, rowdy classes. "Friday was a trying day in school. I know not what method to use to get my children to become more interested in their lessons."

Although Ida didn't enjoy teaching in the classroom, she led a lively social life. As a teacher in the city, she met and made friends with more people. Her weekends were filled with picnics, church fairs, weddings, horseback riding, and afternoon visits with friends. At night Ida attended concerts and the theater. She also took in as much learning as she could—taking speech lessons, attending lectures, and attending church services on Sundays. She loved her speech lessons and would get upset if she had to miss one.

While Ida enjoyed her social life, the railroad suit was troubling her. After months of delay, Ida discovered that the railroad had paid off her lawyer to stop the case from going to court. Since the lawyer was black, Ida had felt sure that he would support her.

Ida was furious. It was bad enough having white people humiliate her on the train. But the actions of the black lawyer—one of her own people—was a greater insult.

Ida did not give up, though. She hired a white lawyer, and the case was heard by Judge Pierce, a former Union soldier. Ida was awarded five hundred dollars. On December 25, 1884, the *Memphis Daily Appeal* printed the following headline: "A Darky Damsel Obtains a Verdict for Damages against the Chesapeake & Ohio Railroad— What It Cost to Put a Colored School Teacher in a Smoking Car—Verdict for $500."

By 1885 Aunt Fannie moved to Visalia, California, with her children and brought Annie and Lily along, too. Ida stayed in Memphis and boarded with a black family. She continued to lead an active social life, mingling with successful black professionals—teachers, doctors, businesspeople, and ministers.

Ida also joined a lecture group, the Memphis Lyceum, which gave her particular pleasure. The talks reminded her of the programs she had enjoyed at school in Holly Springs. Ida especially liked the closing exercises, which included a reading from the *Evening Star,* a newsletter written by the lyceum members. In her diary, Ida referred to this newsletter as a "spicy journal."

The people whom Ida met at the lyceum realized that

she was a talented woman. When the editor of the *Evening Star* left his job, Ida was offered the position. Ida was surprised but delighted and soon discovered that she enjoyed writing. Then one Friday evening, the publisher of the *Living Way,* a weekly black church newspaper, heard Ida read at the lyceum meeting and invited her to write an article for his paper.

She wrote about her experience with the railroad for the *Living Way,* and the editor was impressed with the piece. He asked Ida to write a weekly column, which she agreed to do. She signed her column "Iola." Ida was eager to tell her story to fellow blacks. She wanted to encourage others to stand up for their rights.

At first Ida was unsure of her abilities as a writer. She had no formal training and didn't think she had any talent. "I think sometimes I can write a readable article," she wrote in her diary. "And then again I wonder how I could have been so mistaken in myself."

But Ida did have a gift for writing. She was an observant woman who looked at the conditions of the people around her. She thought about the everyday problems she saw and gave advice in language people could understand.

The black community welcomed her articles. They read them during family and religious gatherings, in barbershops, and at pool halls. Her articles were reprinted in other black newspapers. She was also asked to contribute to important black newspapers like the *New York Freeman* and the *Chicago Conservator.*

When Ida learned of an injustice, it was difficult for her to remain silent. One day she learned of a black woman who was accused of killing a white woman. She found out that the black woman had not received a trial but was murdered instead. In her diary, Ida wrote: "A colored woman accused of poisoning a white one was taken from the county jail and stripped naked and hung up in the courthouse yard and her body riddled with bullets and left exposed to view!"

Ida wrote an article of protest about this incident in the *Gate City Press*. As Ida saw it, there wasn't much evidence against the black woman. But after she wrote the article, Ida wasn't sure she had done the right thing. Her doubts spilled into her diary: "It may be unwise to express myself so strongly but I cannot help it."

Although Ida had doubts about expressing her views, she continued to write and quickly became known for her daring words. Her voice was sweet, and she had a girlish look, yet she was a powerhouse with a pen. She soon gained a reputation as an intelligent woman with a quick temper and outspoken ways.

Ida's honest and critical words sometimes caused her trouble—not only when writing. As a young woman, she had difficulty getting close to some of her women friends. Most women her age were getting married and having babies. But Ida was not interested in getting married. She didn't share common concerns with the women who were wives and mothers.

Ida had gentlemen callers who said they loved her. But she could not return the men's affections, because she didn't want to lose her independence. Even though she was surrounded by people most days, there were times she felt lonely. "Had no visitors today," she wrote one day in 1886. "I don't know what's the matter with me, I feel so dissatisfied with my life, so isolated from all my kind. I cannot or do not make friends."

But Ida did make some friends. Tom and Betty Moss soon became Ida's closest friends in Memphis. Tom was a postman and was trying to save money to open a grocery store. When Tom and Betty had a daughter, they named her Maurine and asked Ida to be her godmother. Ida was delighted.

While Ida struggled with her desire for independence, she also struggled with family obligations. In the summer of 1886, Ida joined her Aunt Fannie and sisters in Visalia, California. There she taught in a one-room schoolhouse for blacks. Ida knew that her aunt could use help caring for the girls. But Visalia was a hot, dusty place. It was a small California town with only a dozen black families. Ida's feet and hands swelled each day after doing household chores. She was cut off from social and educational events. And it was difficult for Ida to write in Visalia. She reluctantly said good-bye to her aunt and her sister Annie. Bringing her eleven-year-old sister Lily with her, Ida returned to Memphis and her teaching job.

When Ida was in her mid-twenties and was still not married, some people who didn't like Ida and what she wrote began saying nasty things about her. Some spread the lie that Lily was not her sister but her daughter.

While Ida struggled with this rumor, she also struggled with money problems. When she was teaching, she didn't always receive her pay on time. And while her writing brought her recognition, it didn't pay much. She tried to send ten dollars a month to Aunt Fannie and occasionally sent something to her two brothers, Jim and George. But Ida had many expenses, and sometimes she spent too much on her clothing.

Clothes were important to Ida. She wanted to act and to look like a lady, with a fan, hat, and gloves. At times Ida's diary revealed her spending habits: "I bought enough silk to finish my dress with, and buttons, thread, linings, etc., amounting to $15.80 and yet have no parasol or other things I would like to have."

But her money problems and family obligations were not enough to distract Ida from the racial tension and increasing limits on the things black people could do. Southern whites were continuing to press for segregation.

As the Reconstruction era ended, Southern states passed Jim Crow laws—laws keeping blacks apart from whites. Railroad cars, restaurants, theaters, streetcars, parks, and playgrounds all had separate sections for blacks and whites.

As more states passed the Jim Crow laws, Tennessee's Supreme Court reheard Ida's case with the Chesapeake & Ohio Railroad. This time the court said that the railroad had done nothing wrong by dragging Ida from the ladies' car.

This was a sickening blow to Ida. On April 11, 1887, she wrote in her diary: "I felt so disappointed because I had hoped such great things from my suit for my people." How could Ida believe there would ever be full freedom and justice for her people? It seemed as if her hopeful dreams were being shoveled into a grave. But Ida had

Ida loved beautiful clothes. She often struggled with her desire to buy fine clothes while she helped support her family.

faith in God. "O God," she prayed in her diary, "is there no redress, no peace, no justice in this land for us? . . . Come to my aid at this moment and teach me what to do."

A week later, it seemed that her prayers were answered. She attended a meeting of the Negro's Mutual Protective Association at the Avery Chapel African Methodist Episcopal (A.M.E.) Church. The association was organized to work for civil rights and to stop white violence.

Ida was excited and encouraged by the sincere and enthusiastic speech by Reverend Benjamin Imes. She was excited to hear a black leader speak of unity. Ida knew that blacks had to work together if they wanted to improve conditions. As soon as Ida returned home, she rushed to her diary and wrote: "The Negro is beginning to think for himself."

After the uplifting speech by Reverend Imes, Ida heard a talk given by Edward Shaw, a black businessman. Shaw was a powerful speaker who also wanted to work for change. Like Ida, he wanted to stir up people. They both knew that black people weren't put on earth to serve and obey whites. And they both wanted their people to take action. Ida had reason to dust off her dreams and keep hoping.

5

A Rude Awakening

In 1889 Ida bought a one-third interest in the *Free Speech and Headlight.* This newspaper was also owned by journalist J. L. Fleming and Reverend Taylor Nightingale, the pastor of the largest black church in Tennessee. Ida continued to speak her mind through this paper. She wrote encouraging words, explaining to readers how their lives would be better if they worked hard and saved money. She also wrote angry words about people who were not honest or who were too timid to fight for change.

In one article, she had harsh words for black schools. She said that the few buildings were not acceptable and that the teachers were poor examples for the children. The article angered the school board so much that Ida was not asked to teach the next year.

Ida was not surprised by the school board's action, but she was shocked to learn that the students' parents did not support her. Ida thought that the parents would want her to speak out on their children's behalf. She thought they would thank her. But they did not. They thought she should have known she would be fired. Ida could not believe that black parents wouldn't want the best for their children.

But a movement to "stir up the people" was slowly taking shape. T. Thomas Fortune, editor of the *New York Age,* formerly the *New York Freeman,* suggested that blacks form a national Afro-American League. Ida loved the idea. The league wanted to "agitate" and wage a war against discrimination, and so did Ida. In 1891 she spoke at the league's second convention in Knoxville, Tennessee.

Protest! Protest! Force the country to see the truth. That's what Ida believed. Soon Ida became known as a troublemaker.

Ida protested the loudest when it came to lynching. For years Ida had heard about lynching. She heard how mobs of white men kidnapped black people suspected of a crime from jail. The mobs then hanged the men or shot them before they could receive a fair trial.

When black people in Georgetown, Kentucky, set fire to their town because a black man had been lynched, the *Free Speech and Headlight* praised the action. In an article, the *Free Speech* encouraged black people to protest and defend themselves.

White people were outraged by the article. They accused the *Free Speech* of encouraging hate and violence.

They blamed Reverend Nightingale, Ida's newspaper partner, for the article and decided to punish him. They convinced some of his former church members to accuse him of assault, and then they convicted Nightingale of the crime. Nightingale fled to Oklahoma.

With Nightingale gone, Ida and J. L. Fleming were left as co-owners of the newspaper. Ida intended to keep printing eye-opening articles. She planned to expand the circulation of the paper. She traveled to neighboring states to attract new readers, and soon the number of copies sold more than doubled.

Then on March 9, 1892, while Ida was gone, her friend Tom Moss was lynched. He had opened a grocery store—the People's Grocery Company—with Calvin McDowell and Henry Stewart. The white grocer in the area had become angry when the People's Grocery opened. Black customers had started shopping at Tom's store, and the white grocer had lost business.

The white grocer had been looking for an opportunity to start trouble and put an end to the People's Grocery. His opportunity came one day when some black boys got into an argument with a group of white boys during a game of marbles. The boys' fathers got involved, and the situation worsened. Tom was warned that a white mob was going to attack his store. He and his business partners knew they had no choice but to protect themselves with guns. At about ten o'clock on a Saturday night, a group of white men approached the back door of the People's Grocery. Shots rang out, and three white men were wounded.

Tom and his partners were arrested. Four days after the shooting, the three men were dragged from the city jail before dawn, carried a mile north on a railroad engine, and shot.

Ida was outraged when she read about the lynching in a Memphis newspaper. She hurried home to Memphis to be with Tom's wife and daughter.

Ida was saddened and angered by the news of Tom's lynching. She knew that Tom would never commit a crime. She was sure that Tom and his partners must have had no choice but to protect themselves with guns. Tom was an honest, hardworking man. His murder was a shock to Ida. Even though the white grocer had lost business to the People's Grocery, Ida had had no reason to think Tom would ever be murdered. Many blacks in Memphis had fine homes and were involved in a variety of businesses. As far as Ida knew, Tom's murder was the first lynching of a black business owner in Memphis.

The black community in Memphis was just as stunned as Ida. Groups gathered at the grocery and around town to discuss what had happened. But as soon as the judge heard of these group meetings, he ordered the sheriff and his men to shoot any blacks who looked like they were making trouble.

After the judge's order, it wasn't long before white mobs were recklessly shooting into groups of peaceful blacks. Then whites raided the People's Grocery, stole the food, and destroyed the property. The message they sent the black community was loud and clear.

When Ida heard of these events, she knew what she had

to do. She couldn't bring Tom back from the dead, but she had to lead her people in protest.

Ida now realized that lynching was a way of frightening and controlling blacks. So she wrote a feature article for the *Free Speech*. Echoing Tom's last words, she told black families to leave town. She felt that there was no future for black people in Memphis. Black people would

Tom Moss's lynching set Ida into action on a crusade to stop lynching and mistreatment of blacks. She is pictured with Tom's wife, Betty *(center)*, and Tom and Betty's two children.

not get fair trials in court. They would not be allowed to protect themselves with guns. It seemed that whites would kill any black who became too successful. Ida told black people to stop shopping in the city's white-owned stores and to stop riding the city's streetcars. She urged them to save their money and move West.

Her words proved more powerful than any gun. Within two months, six thousand black people followed Ida's advice and left the city.

White businesspeople were shocked. White store owners lost money as their black customers left town. White housewives could no longer find black servants to clean their houses and sweat over their hot stoves. And there was nothing white people could do about it.

Six weeks after the lynching, the managers of the Memphis streetcar company came to the office of the

Ida encouraged blacks to settle in Oklahoma. This black family settled near Guthrie, Oklahoma, in 1889.

Free Speech to beg Ida to persuade black riders to use the streetcars. This was an interesting turn of events. Ida knew she had the upper hand with these two men. She asked them why they thought black people had stopped riding the cars.

The two men did not want to face the truth—that the lynching of Tom Moss had caused their problem—so instead they said that they thought blacks were afraid of electricity. When Ida reminded them that their jobs depended on the black customer, the men turned red with embarrassment.

Ida made it clear to the two men that blacks had stopped riding the streetcars because of Moss's lynching. Ida and the other blacks in town knew that black people were not allowed to serve on juries. A jury of white men would never convict whites of the crime. Ida also suspected that the judge himself was involved in Moss's murder.

The managers continued to plead with Ida and to promise that blacks would be treated with every courtesy if they again rode the streetcars. But Ida wasn't swayed. She knew the lynchers would never be punished. So when the streetcar managers left, she wrote about her meeting with them and again asked black riders to stay off the cars.

During the weeks that followed, the white press in Memphis tried to stop the westward movement of black families to Oklahoma. They tried to scare black families by telling them that blacks were starving out West, the weather was harsh, and Indians of the region were dangerous. Ida suspected the white press was lying. So she took a three-week trip to explore various parts of Oklahoma. She sent letters back to the *Free Speech,* letting her readers know of the opportunities to own land. In fact, she would have moved to Oklahoma herself. But J. L. Fleming, her business partner, did not want to move the *Free Speech* to Oklahoma.

During the months following Tom's lynching, Ida did some investigative reporting about lynching. For some time she had wondered about all the black men who had been accused of raping white women and had then been lynched. Maybe these men hadn't really attacked women, after all. Ida traveled throughout the South to dig up more information about the lynching of accused rapists that she was reading about in the paper.

Ida talked to people who knew of the supposed attacks. She talked to one white woman who had supposedly been attacked by a black man when she was a young girl. The woman admitted that she had not been raped. In other cases, Ida spoke to relatives of lynching victims. They told her about white women who, after their accused rapists had been lynched, admitted they had not been raped after all.

Many white people in Memphis grew to despise Ida's strong words on racial matters. These whites blamed her for black people leaving Memphis and hurting white business. These white leaders planned to get rid of Ida and the *Free Speech.* But they needed an excuse to avoid angering the few blacks who were left in town.

At the end of May 1892, Ida published an editorial in the *Free Speech.* Using the facts she had gathered, Ida

Nineteen-year-old Abram Smith *(left)* and eighteen-year-old Thomas Shipp *(right)* were taken from a jail and hanged from a tree in a public square after they had been accused of murdering Claude Deeter and assaulting his girlfriend, Mary Ball.

boldly stated that no one believed all the reports of black men attacking white women. She said the reports were lies. She hinted that the white women had been attracted to the black men and had fallen in love with them.

When white readers saw Ida's editorial, they were furious. Most white people did not want to believe that white women could love black men. Many believed that only white men could be attracted to and fall in love with black women.

After Ida's article appeared, a group of white men destroyed the office of the *Free Speech*. They used the excuse that they were defending the honor of white women. Ida was traveling along the East Coast when the attack took place. She was scheduled to meet with T. Thomas Fortune in New Jersey. As soon as Ida saw Fortune, he handed her a paper with the shocking news about the office.

Ida was relieved to know that her partner J. L. Fleming had escaped safely from the city. But Fleming blamed Ida for the destruction of the *Free Speech*, and she lost her friendship with him. She also lost her home. She received letters and telegrams from friends telling her that white men were watching the trains and planned to hang her in front of the courthouse if she came back! Ida could not return to Memphis.

6

SOUTHERN HORRORS
AND SHAME

Although Ida lost her paper and her home, she realized she would have the freedom to tell the whole truth about lynching. Being in the North gave her the opportunity to answer a question she had often asked herself.

For a long time, Ida had wondered why the North was silent about lynching. She wondered if Northerners didn't know the facts. Maybe Northerners believed the lies printed in the white press—that those who had been lynched *had* committed violent crimes.

T. Thomas Fortune helped Ida by inviting her to join his paper, the *New York Age,* and Ida began writing a two-column article each week. Her first writing experience for the *Age* was a special event. On June 25, 1892, the paper printed her story on the front page. Ida signed the piece, "Exiled." She gave names, dates, and places of people who had been accused of rape and then lynched. The *Age* printed ten thousand copies of this issue and distributed them throughout the country, including the South. In Memphis alone, one thousand copies were sold.

Ida hoped that white Northerners would notice her article and comment about it in the white press. But they didn't. As far as Ida knew, only one white person reacted to her article. A lawyer, Judge Albion W. Tourgee, condemned lynching in the weekly column he wrote for the *Chicago Inter-Ocean,* a white newspaper.

The most impressive reaction to her article came from the leading black reformer, Frederick Douglass. He made a special trip from his home in Washington, D.C., to meet with her. He praised her work and said he hadn't been aware of the facts about lynching until he read her article.

This meeting with Frederick Douglass was a special moment in Ida's life. Like most black people, she thought he was the greatest black leader in the country. She was enlivened by his encouraging words and became friends with him and his wife, Helen Pitts.

While Ida admired Frederick Douglass, he in turn appreciated the kind manner in which Ida treated his wife. Helen was white, and many black women who visited the Douglass home treated her coldly and rudely.

Ida also found support for her writings on lynching from two black women from New York—Victoria Earle Matthews and Maritcha Lyons. They organized a group of women to gather at Lyric Hall in New York City on October 5, 1892, to show their support of Ida.

When Ida entered the hall, she found the room crowded and her pen name "Iola" spelled out in electric lights above the speaker's platform. Leading black women

Frederick Douglass and his wife, Helen Pitts Douglass, at Niagara Falls on their honeymoon

from Boston and Philadelphia were there, and miniature copies of the *Free Speech* were handed out as programs. After music and speeches, Victoria Matthews introduced Ida to the audience.

Ida left her handkerchief on her seat and approached the speaker's platform. She looked out at the women gathered before her. Suddenly she felt frightened. She had never given an address to such a large crowd, and at that moment, she felt lonely and homesick for her Memphis friends. But she forced herself to tell the story of Tom Moss's lynching, tears streaming down her cheeks.

Ida's voice remained steady, but she felt foolish crying in front of everyone and wanted desperately to wipe away the tears. She slipped her hand behind her and

Lynchings drew large crowds in the South.

waved for her handkerchief. Then, without skipping a word, she wiped her nose and face.

Although Ida was angry at herself—she thought crying in public was a sign of weakness—the audience was moved by her words. They wanted her to continue her crusade against lynching. They gave her a pen-shaped gold brooch and five hundred dollars to help in her work.

Ida used the money to expand her June *New York Age* article into a pamphlet entitled *Southern Horrors*. People from around the country had urged Ida to produce such a pamphlet, and it opened with a letter from Frederick Douglass. In the letter, Mr. Douglass called Ida a brave woman and said that her words against lynching had been the most powerful outcry on the subject.

Ida's words were powerful because they were true. In *Southern Horrors,* Ida wrote that the South had not changed much after the Civil War. She pointed out that white Southerners still did not want blacks to be free, to vote, or to enjoy all the rights that white people had.

Ida acknowledged that some white Southerners did not approve of lynching. In a few cases, attempts were made to give accused black rapists fair trials and guard them against lynching mobs. But there was no outcry to stop lynching. Too many white men and women remained silent. Ida believed these silent men and women were just as guilty as the lawbreakers who did the lynching.

Ida felt that white society would never admit that it was doing anything wrong in lynching black people and in treating them unfairly in many other ways. Her strategy for change was to hurt white people financially. The white man loves money more than anything else, she declared. Whites would only stop killing blacks if the murders meant losing money, she felt. If there was a lynching in a town, Ida urged black people to stop spending money at the town's white businesses. She told black people to stop spending money on cigars, drinks, and shoe shines. Let whites lose money, she believed. Then they would listen.

In her writings, Ida also reminded blacks that the South couldn't thrive without black labor. Because of this, black people did have the power to change society with their actions.

After her appearance at Lyric Hall, Ida had even more speaking engagements. Groups of black women were forming clubs, and they asked Ida to speak to them. Invitations came from Wilmington, Delaware; Chester, Pennsylvania; Philadelphia; and Washington, D.C. In Boston, Ida spoke before her first white audience.

In each city, Ida pointed out that most people thought that lynching occurred after a man was accused of attacking a woman. With information from white newspapers, Ida showed that only one-third of those lynched were even charged with attacking women.

The fact was, many black men were lynched for robbery, arguing with white men, or making threats. She pointed out that in 1891, one black man had been lynched because he was drunk and merely talked back to some white people.

While Ida toured the Northern states, the white newspapers in Memphis followed her activities and looked for ways to discredit her. One paper falsely reported that she had had a love affair with the Reverend Nightingale, her former *Free Speech* partner.

Ida was upset by this lie, not just because it damaged her reputation but because she felt it hurt the reputation of all black women. She inquired about suing the newspaper that had printed the lies. She asked Judge Tourgee for his opinion of the matter. He was busy preparing another case, but he recommended Ferdinand Barnett, a black attorney in Chicago. Ida and Ferdinand Barnett wrote to each other in preparation for the lawsuit. But other events kept them busy, and Ida forgot about suing the newspaper.

While Ida was giving speeches about lynching, people

all over the United States were making plans for a cele-bration—the four hundredth anniversary of Columbus's voyage to America. A world's fair, known as the World's Columbian Exposition, would be held in Chicago in May 1893. People from all over the world would attend.

There would be many buildings at the exposition. Each state would have the chance to set up an exhibit in a building. Since the buildings were white on the outside, the fairgrounds were called "The White City."

Like other black people, Ida saw the Columbian Expo-sition as a way to show the world what the black commu-nity had achieved since the end of the Civil War. But black people were not included on the planning committees and would not be represented at the exposi-tion. Outraged, Frederick Douglass and Ida decided that foreign visitors should know about the accomplishments of black people. They should know why black people were not represented at the fair. They planned to ask the black community for the five thousand dollars needed for Ida to print a booklet. Sections of the eighty-one page booklet were to be written by Ida B. Wells, Frederick Douglass, and the Chicago lawyer Ferdinand L. Barnett. The booklet was called *The Reason Why the Colored American Is Not in the World's Columbian Exposition.*

Ida had hoped that the booklet would be printed in French, German, Spanish, and English. But Frederick had difficulty raising money. Many black editors criti-cized Ida and Frederick. The editors admitted there was racial discrimination in this country. But they thought that telling foreign visitors about lynching and injustice would only make black people feel disgraced. These editors didn't think that foreigners could help the situation. They also feared that the booklet would anger white Americans, and they felt that contributing to it was a waste of money. So the twenty thousand copies of the booklet that were printed were written in English, with introductions in French and German.

The Columbian Exposition divided black leaders in other ways. Since black people had not been included in the planning stage, some of the leaders thought that black people should set up their own exhibit, separate from the other buildings. But the managers of the fair ruled against racially separate exhibits.

At this same time, news reports of a horrible lynching in Paris, Texas, came out. In the small Texas town, a black man had been accused of killing a five-year-old. The man had not been given a trial but had been burned alive in front of a cheering crowd. When Isabelle Mayo of Scotland and Catherine Impey of England heard of it, they were outraged. Catherine Impey, who was fighting to end mistreatment of poor people in India, knew of Ida's work. She and Isabelle Mayo invited Ida to come to Great Britain in the spring of 1893 and speak about lynching in the United States.

In those days, it was unusual for a single woman to travel abroad alone. But that didn't stop Ida. She boarded a ship with another single woman, Dr. Georgia Patton, the first black female doctor in Memphis. The two weathered the rough journey together, overwhelmed by seasickness.

Once she arrived in Scotland, Ida's tour began with meetings in Isabelle's home. Ida told the lynching stories to the influential people who gathered. Isabelle was impressed and excited by the way Ida presented the facts. Ida quickly got the people's attention and soon found herself speaking before larger audiences. One evening she spoke before a crowd of fifteen hundred people.

Ida then went to England, where she talked about segregation in the United States. She told her audiences that whites hired blacks as servants in their homes, but they didn't allow blacks to enter their hotels and concert halls. The audiences were surprised to learn that white Christians in the southern United States forced black people to sit in the back of their churches. Ida told her listeners that it was impossible for a black person to receive a fair trial in the United States since the judges, juries, sheriffs, and jailers were all white.

Ida told the British crowds that killing a black person was often not considered a crime in the United States. She brought newspaper accounts and photographs of black men hanging with nooses around their necks.

The British people were shocked to see people dangling from ropes. They were even more horrified to see the young children in the pictures staring up at the lifeless bodies.

Ida told of the carnival atmosphere that surrounded some lynchings. Some white mobs treated these killings as festive occasions, Ida told them. Before some lynchings, local newspapers announced the upcoming event, and children were given a holiday so they could attend.

Rubin Stacy was lynched in Fort Lauderdale, Florida, because his killers said he frightened a white woman.

In the lynching in Paris, Texas, the accused black man had been paraded through the streets on a float. Then a fire had been started and red-hot irons had been used to burn the man's body. A crowd of ten thousand people had cheered as the poor man cried out in agony.

Ida asked the British to condemn lynching. Ida didn't think Americans could ignore the problem if the British spoke out. Ida had good reason to believe that the British would support her. In Great Britain, black people were treated with respect. They were welcomed on all public transportation, in theaters, hotels, churches, and restaurants. According to Ida, British whites truly enjoyed the company of black people.

7

WATERMELONS AND BICKERING

In May 1893, the same month that Ida returned from her trip overseas, the Columbian Exposition opened in Chicago. Ida was not looking forward to the event. The exposition managers had announced that one day of the fair would be set aside as "Colored American Day." Other days had been set aside as special celebration days for Swedes, Germans, Irish, and other nationalities. The idea of "Colored American Day" infuriated Ida. Fair officials were planning to provide two thousand watermelons for that day. In those days, white cartoonists drew pictures of black characters slobbering over watermelons. The cartoons were meant to insult blacks.

Ida wanted the world to see that many black Americans were refined and educated. She cringed at the thought of crowds of blacks racing to get free watermelon, munching on the juicy fruit and spitting seeds, with the juices dribbling down their chins. A sight like that could only lower the whites' image of blacks, Ida thought. This event would give whites another reason for not treating blacks as equals.

Hundreds of thousands of people attended the Columbian Exposition in Chicago in 1893. On August 25, fairgoers got to hear Frederick Douglass speak.

Many newspapers supported Ida's views. But Frederick Douglass disagreed with her. He thought it was wise to accept the day and use it to show white people that black people were educated and refined in speech and behavior.

During the fair, Ida distributed her booklet at the Haitian Pavilion, where Frederick was in charge. But on August 25, Colored American Day, Ida chose not to participate in the celebration.

That day, the watermelons were brought in and a cartoonist was on hand to make drawings of the black fairgoers. But white visitors to the fair did not see blacks rushing for free watermelon. They saw a dignified crowd of black citizens participating in a formal afternoon program. Singers gave a concert, and Frederick Douglass gave a major speech. He pointed out that while the country had almost eight million blacks—about one-tenth of the U.S. population—they were not represented fairly by the Columbian Exposition.

When Ida heard about his speech, she was sorry she had not been at the fair that day. She felt she had made a mistake. She rushed to Frederick and apologized.

During the months-long Columbian Exposition, a group of black men started a club—the Tourgee Club—as a place to entertain black visitors to the fair. Black women were invited to the club every Thursday, which had been set aside as ladies' day. But not many women came. So Ida was asked to speak as a way of attracting ladies to the club.

During her talks, Ida told the women about the black women's clubs in the East and women's clubs in England. She told them that as an organized group, she felt they could force changes in society. Soon after, Ida helped form a permanent black women's club in Chicago. The club became known as the Ida B. Wells Club.

The club met every week, attracting female black leaders, teachers, housewives, and high-school girls. It sponsored lectures, discussions, and musical programs, often by important and well-known people.

By this time, Ida had decided to make Chicago her home. She took a job writing for the *Chicago Conservator,* the oldest black paper in the city. Ferdinand L. Barnett was the editor and founder of the paper. Ida had many things in common with Ferdinand, a widower with two young sons, and she found him attractive.

Like Ida, Ferdinand wanted the best for black people and worked hard for civil rights. Like Ida, he was a refined, well-educated person. Ferdinand was an attorney who believed in doing what was right, managing money wisely, and bringing different racial groups together. And

Ferdinand Barnett was a well-known, successful attorney when he met Ida B. Wells.

like Ida, he believed that successful black people should help the less fortunate of their race. He believed black leaders should put aside their differences and jealousies and work together. Ida felt right at home working for him on the *Conservator.*

In January 1894, W. T. Stead, an English editor, gave a rousing and controversial speech at the Ida B. Wells Club. He scolded black people in the United States for not uniting and working together. Shockingly honest like Ida, he told the women that maybe black people hadn't been lynched enough. Ida welcomed his agitating words and hoped they would spark the women into action.

Later in 1894, Ida made a second trip to England. She retold terrifying accounts of lynching. During that tour, she wrote about her experiences in a column titled "Ida B. Wells Abroad," which appeared in the *Chicago Inter-Ocean.*

As a result of her work, several British groups condemned lynching. The London Anti-Lynching Committee was formed, which included many famous English people. British newspapers supported Ida's work. But she learned that the *Memphis Daily Commercial* had blasted the British people for believing Ida. In one issue, the newspaper devoted four columns to an attack on Ida's character—hoping to persuade the British that Ida was lying. But the language in the Memphis newspaper was so crude and disgusting that British people saw the article as proof that she was telling the truth.

Ida addressed clubs, parlor meetings, breakfast and dinner parties in London, continuing to hope that Americans would talk publicly about the lynching problem the way the British were doing. Surely Americans could not ignore the British people's strong response, Ida thought.

Then at an evening party in London, a guest read an open letter to Ida from the citizens of California. The letter extended an invitation to Ida to come and speak in California about lynching. It was a glimmer of hope.

With that hope, Ida returned to the United States to work on the *Conservator* and to tour cities in the North, traveling from the Atlantic Ocean to the Pacific. Ida had hoped that the black community would support her speaking engagements by donating money. This way, she would not have to charge a fee for her appearances. But many black people were poor and could not help. Few of those who could afford to give money did. So Ida began charging a fee.

In addition to speaking to black audiences, Ida appeared at many white churches and gatherings. She asked white people to follow the example of the British people and support her efforts to stop the lynching. Ida was pleased with the positive response from white crowds. She felt her message about lynching was finally going to make a difference.

But after meeting with several white church groups in Philadelphia, Ida appeared before a group of black ministers. After her speech, one minister praised the work Ida had done. But another minister, Reverend Doctor Embry, rose with a different opinion. He said he wasn't sure the ministers should support Ida and her crusade against lynching. One or two others agreed with Embry.

Ida was insulted. While white ministers enthusiastically supported her work, black ministers questioned what she was doing. Telling them she didn't need their help—that she had God's help—she walked out of the meeting.

Ida was troubled to see her own people oppose her. She couldn't understand it, since the British people had rallied around her. But Ida never backed down for anything or anyone—whether it was strangers or people she admired and considered friends.

Susan B. Anthony was one of the people Ida admired and considered a friend. Susan was a pioneer in the women's rights movement, demanding that women be allowed to vote. She knew that women needed the vote in order to make changes in society. Susan also campaigned against drunkenness and slavery, so her path often crossed Ida's.

Susan could be as outspoken as Ida. One time, Ida and Susan attended a women's rights meeting in Rochester, New York. A young man from the audience asked Ida why more blacks didn't come to the North if they were so badly treated in the South.

Susan rose to her feet before Ida could speak. She pointed out that Northerners didn't treat blacks much better than Southerners did. Ida had witnessed segregation in the North—in schools, churches, hotels, and social gatherings—and knew that Susan was right.

After the meeting in Rochester, Ida stayed at Susan's house. Susan told Ida that she could use the services of her secretary, but the secretary refused to work for Ida

Susan B. Anthony became a close friend of Ida's.

because Ida was black. When Susan discovered this, she fired the young woman. Susan's actions showed Ida her commitment to justice for blacks.

Susan B. Anthony's strongest efforts went toward getting women the right to vote. She felt that the National Women's Suffrage Association needed women from the North and the South to unite in the fight. But when the organization held a convention in Atlanta, Georgia Susan did not ask Frederick Douglass—an honorary member of the association—to join them. Susan was afraid Frederick would be insulted by white Southerners. And she did not want to offend Southern women by the presence of a black leader. She wanted Southern women to join the association.

Ida thought that Susan was wrong not to invite Frederick. She expressed her fear that even though Susan was helping women get the vote, she was helping to continue segregation.

But Ida still thought of Susan as a dear friend. Susan treated Ida with respect and kindness and was eager to listen to Ida's opinion. Ida appreciated this and realized that Susan had a different way of working for justice. She believed that once women got the right to vote, they would vote to make changes to improve life for black people. But Ida was not as optimistic. She didn't believe white women's votes would change anything for blacks.

On February 20, 1895, Ida had one more reason to be less optimistic. Frederick Douglass died at his home in Washington, D.C. Ida was in San Francisco at the time. She was saddened when she heard the news that her good friend, and one of America's finest leaders, was dead. She was even more upset when she realized she was too far away to attend the funeral. Wanting to honor him in some way, she held a memorial service for him in San Francisco.

Soon after she returned to Chicago, she had a happy event to brighten her life. On June 27, 1895, a few weeks before her thirty-third birthday, Ida B. Wells married Ferdinand L. Barnett. The wedding day was a splendid occasion in Chicago. The Ida B. Wells Club took care of all the arrangements, which included a reception after the church service. Hundreds of friends and strangers gathered for the affair, and Ida's sisters traveled from California to be her bridesmaids.

Ida was a beautiful bride in her dress of white satin trimmed with chiffon and orange blossoms. She and Ferdinand enjoyed a carriage ride to the church through streets crowded with well-wishers. They received congratulations in two large parlors decorated with ferns, palms, and roses.

But when news of Ida's marriage spread across the country, black people protested. They felt that Ida had deserted their cause by choosing to marry. Newspapers voiced their disapproval of her marriage.

Ida was upset when she heard about the protests. She felt that black people wanted her to raise her voice and fight for fair treatment of blacks. They wanted her to devote her life to crusade for justice. But when Ida had asked for their support, these same blacks had not helped. She felt she had not deserted the cause—they had deserted her.

8

WIFE, MOTHER, AND "HOTHEAD"

When Ida married Ferdinand, she became Ida B. Wells-Barnett. She kept the name "Wells" so people would remember who she was and what she had accomplished. Ferdinand was a widower and had two sons— eleven-year-old Ferdinand Jr. and nine-year-old Albert. Ferdinand's mother lived with them and helped with the boys. Ida wanted to keep pouring her energy into her work, so she was happy to have her mother-in-law live with them and keep house.

After her wedding, Ida focused her energy on the *Conservator,* which she had bought before her marriage. She also spent time speaking to white women's clubs in Chicago and became president of the Ida B. Wells Club.

The club tackled many projects, including opening a kindergarten. In the 1890s, kindergartens were a new thing. Ida wanted to make sure black children had a chance to go to kindergarten. So the Ida B. Wells Club proposed starting a kindergarten in Bethel A.M.E. Church, a black church in Ida's neighborhood. But some leading black citizens were not very enthusiastic about

The Ida B. Wells Club organized the opening of a kindergarten in a black church.

this plan. They wanted their children to go to a nearby white kindergarten where the waiting list was long. Black children would have to wait to enroll there.

Even though Ida liked the idea of black children learning with white children, she couldn't understand why some black people were against her plan. Ida thought it was more important to help the black children immediately. She didn't think it made sense to wait for the white kindergarten to accept black students.

With the support of Bethel Church's pastor, Ida and her club opened their kindergarten in the church. It was not a kindergarten just for black children. It was a school where any child in the neighborhood was welcome to attend.

During the first year of her marriage, Ida was active in the community. But when black women's clubs across the country decided to meet in Boston to form a national club, Ida was too exhausted to attend. By that time, she was pregnant with her son, Charles, who was born in 1896. Ida was determined to be a good mother, but juggling her roles as a mother and crusader was difficult.

Ida did attend the club's second meeting in Washington, D.C., in the summer of 1896. She was there with four-month-old Charles in her arms. At this meeting, the group decided to call itself the National Association of Colored Women.

A few months later, during the 1896 election campaigns, a women's committee asked Ida to tour Illinois and speak in support of the Republican Party. Part of Ida was hoping she wouldn't have to make the tour. She told the committee that a nurse would have to travel with her

Ida B. Wells-Barnett and her firstborn son, Charles Akid Barnett

to care for Charles. Ida knew the committee didn't have money to hire a nurse. But to Ida's surprise, the committee promised that a nurse would be at each stop. Ida was off once again.

In 1897, Ida gave birth to another son, Herman. By

this time, Ida decided that she wanted to retire from public life and devote her energy to her children. Ida felt a great responsibility to Charles and Herman. Ida thought it was important to train them properly when they were young. And she thought it was her job to do this, not her husband's or her mother-in-law's. (Ida's mother-in-law and stepsons had moved into a house nearby about a year after Ida and Ferdinand had married.)

In 1898 a terrible lynching occurred in Anderson, South Carolina. On February 21, a white mob of more than three hundred people set a black postmaster's home on fire. When his family raced out, the mob shot and wounded them. The man was killed inside the house, and his body was left to burn in the flames. His infant son was also killed.

Since the man worked for the U.S. government, some citizens of Chicago hoped that the government would punish the lynchers. Ida knew she had to help. Black Chicagoans collected money for Ida to travel to Washington, D.C. So once again Ida was off, leaving Charles with her husband and his mother and bringing five-month-old Herman with her.

Ida arranged an interview with President William McKinley. He listened to her plea to punish the lynchers. She let him know that only a savage country would allow mobs of people to hunt down a lone man and murder him. It was a disgrace that a civilized country like the United States would allow this to happen. President McKinley treated Ida with respect and told her that he would deal with the case.

After speaking with the president, Ida spent five more weeks in Washington. She worked to persuade the U.S. Congress to give some money to the postmaster's widow and children to support them. But during this time, Congress declared war on Spain. The government was focused on problems abroad. Ida was told to go home and come back in December.

While home, Ida hoped the black community would organize and raise money for her return trip to Washington. But once again, Ida was sadly disappointed. The money never came. In fact, during the first five-week visit to Washington, Ida and her husband had to pay much of the expenses themselves.

Ida brought lynching to the attention of President William McKinley.

Ida knew that if all black people united, the country would be forced to change. Ida was willing to lead her people, but she needed help. When were blacks going to protest *together*!

That autumn, T. Thomas Fortune of the *New York Age* called for a meeting of the Afro-American League in Rochester. During the meeting, the league decided to become the National Afro-American Council.

In Rochester, Ida was again the guest of Susan B. Anthony. During her stay, Susan addressed Ida as Mrs. Barnett. And as Ida said, Susan would "bite out [my] married name." She seemed to disapprove of Ida getting married. After a few days, Ida asked Susan about this.

Susan said that marriage was all right for some women. But she believed that Ida was different from most women. She felt that Ida should devote her life to agitating the nation into bringing justice for blacks. Susan understood that Ida could no longer focus all her energy on the cause. She knew that Ida's thoughts were on her family. Susan pointed out that ever since Ida's marriage, protest concerning the mistreatment of blacks had almost stopped.

Ida understood what Susan was saying. But Ida felt that her friend didn't understand the real problem. Her family wasn't keeping her from her work—she just wasn't getting support from her own people.

Uniting black people was an ongoing problem. When the National Afro-American Council met in Chicago, its members came with different opinions. The members split into two camps—those who backed Booker T. Washington and those who were radicals like Ida.

Booker T. Washington was the founder of the Tuskegee Institute in Alabama. At the institute, black students focused on job training and learning to make a decent living. Booker didn't urge black people to seek political power or to protest for their full civil rights. His ideas appealed to many of the whites who took an interest in helping blacks.

Ida felt that protest was necessary to bring about change. Her experiences convinced her that blacks would not gain justice unless whites were forced to change. The discussion she had had with President McKinley about the black postmaster's lynching had proven her point. Though the president had promised to look into the matter, nothing ever came of the promise.

While Ida saw protest as the only solution, other blacks saw protest as useless. Many blacks decided to accept life as it was and to concentrate on earning a living. They followed Booker's ideas of stressing job training for blacks.

Many of the blacks at the National Afro-American Council labeled Ida a "hothead." Ida wanted the council to prepare a fiery statement to Congress and to the president of the United States. But the statement they prepared was not as strong as Ida had wanted. Even though the council condemned mob violence and supported political activity in the North, it didn't protest for change in the South. It didn't protest Southern laws that kept blacks from voting. It didn't press for the end of Jim Crow segregation laws. Instead it urged blacks to educate themselves and to work hard.

Booker T. Washington was head of Tuskegee Institute for thirty-four years. He also founded the National Negro Business League, established Negro Health Week, and was the first black man elected to the New York University Hall of Fame.

Ida continued to lose support from some of the black community because of her radical ideas and other reasons. Some black leaders were interested in power. Some were jealous of Ida. They did not like the attention she got, and they did not want the black community to follow her.

In 1899, Mary Church Terrell called a meeting of the National Association of Colored Women in Chicago. Mary did not ask for Ida's help with arranging the meeting, and Ida was not asked to speak at the meeting. Ida was hurt. She finally asked Mary why she hadn't been included.

To Ida's surprise, Mary told her that the women of Chicago had written letters saying they would not come to the meeting if Ida was involved. Ida took the news hard. She had helped bring these women into the club, and now they seemed to have turned against her.

As time went on, Ida learned more about the situation. Mary had been using the women's letters as an excuse. She wanted to be reelected as president of the club herself. She didn't want Ida in the spotlight for fear that the women might decide to elect her.

Although Ida was discouraged by these events, she was happy with her growing family. In 1901, her daughter Ida was born. Then in 1904, another girl, Alfreda, was born. With four children of her own, Ida spent even more time at home.

Besides caring for the children, Ida kept busy reading and writing. Ferdinand liked to cook, so he often helped out. Ida didn't like cooking or cleaning the house. She usually hired somebody to do the housework. Ida didn't feel she accomplished anything when she cleaned, because the next day it was dirty again.

The Barnett family was one of the first black families to move into a white neighborhood. They moved to a nice house on Rhodes Avenue. But the neighbors weren't nice. They made it known that they weren't happy about a black family living on their block. When they saw the Barnetts outside, they left their porches, marched into their houses, and slammed their doors.

Ida B. Wells-Barnett and her four children, Charles, Herman, Ida, and Alfreda

9

A Helping Hand and Protest

Many of the black people who moved to Chicago from the South had difficulty finding jobs and housing. Ida felt it was her duty to help them. When Robert T. Motts—a saloon keeper—opened a black theater in the city, Ida supported it. But not everyone in the community supported the theater. They didn't like the idea of a bar owner in their neighborhood.

Since Motts was trying to help blacks, Ida thought that his past as a saloon keeper should be forgiven and people should support his theater. There, blacks would be able to sit anywhere they wanted. There would be an all-black orchestra. And the theater would give blacks a chance to perfect their skills as actors. Ida was able to help raise five hundred dollars to support the theater.

Raising her children kept Ida busy. The children attended schools with white students. Ida often went to the schools to get reports about her children. She expected the reports to be good—she expected her children to work hard.

The Barnetts had an old piano and a Victrola—an early record player. Young Ida took piano lessons, while Alfreda took dance lessons. Ferdinand had a great sense of humor, but Ida did not joke often. Yet once in a while, Ferdinand would turn on the Victrola and play a record called "The Preacher and the Bear." It was a story about a preacher who went hunting. Every time Ida heard the preacher pray, "Now, Lord, if you can't help me / For goodness sake, don't help that bear," she couldn't help laughing.

Ida also loosened up a bit with a game of whist—a card game. She would play whist with the family and with company. People were always dropping by. The Barnett children often shared Sunday afternoons with visitors and took part in the conversations.

Though many blacks moving to Chicago had difficulty just finding jobs, some individuals had the opportunity to own a business. This is a black-owned gunsmith shop in Chicago in 1900.

Happy times were mixed with troubled times. Some of the white boys in the neighborhood formed a gang—the 31st Street gang. Ida's boys and other black boys were often attacked by them.

Ida wasn't about to let anyone touch her boys. One night when the gang chased her sons home, she dared the gang to step past her. Everyone in the neighborhood knew Ida had a gun. She had gotten it when her life was threatened in Memphis. Ida's children never saw the gun and neither did the white gang. Ida's words were enough to keep the gang away. But Ida couldn't stop the increase of violence in Chicago.

In 1908 a riot broke out in Springfield, Illinois. It was said that the riot was sparked by two crimes committed by two black men. In one case, a white person had been murdered. In the other, a white woman had been raped. But most people knew that trouble had been brewing in the city long before these crimes.

As black people moved North in the late 1800s, white people grew angry because they had to compete with blacks for jobs. During three days of rioting in Springfield, white mobs burned black homes and stores. Three innocent blacks were lynched. One was an old man who had been married to a white woman for twenty years. It was clear to many people that whites wanted to drive blacks from the city.

Ida was frustrated. The black community of Chicago didn't seem to be concerned about the riots. The leaders didn't think that they could do anything to help. To prove them wrong, Ida formed the Negro Fellowship League to discuss current events. It first met at her house in 1908 on Sunday afternoons. She started with three men from the Bible class she taught.

The Springfield riots also sparked a group of whites and blacks to form an organization to protect and advance life for black people. It would be called the National Association for the Advancement of Colored People—the NAACP. The NAACP supporters included many white liberals, such as the famous reformer Jane Addams. Leading blacks, such as Ida and W.E.B. DuBois, also supported the group.

Jane Addams was a strong supporter of the National Association for the Advancement of Colored People (NAACP).

Jessie Faucet was the literary editor of the NAACP magazine, *Crisis,* from 1919 until 1926.

At an NAACP meeting in New York City in 1909, Ida spoke about lynching. Along with a few other black members, she wanted the NAACP to present a strong statement to the U.S. government demanding that lawmakers make lynching a national crime. But many of the people at the meeting—most of whom were white— would not agree to that. Instead, the statement to Congress and the president demanded only that civil rights be guaranteed to all people.

In the fall of 1909, Ida heard of another lynching. A white woman was found dead in an alley in Cairo, Illinois. A black homeless man called "Frog" James was arrested for the crime. James never got a trial. The sheriff, Frank Davis, took James out of Cairo when he heard there might be a lynching. But a white mob found James, brought him back to town, and hanged him. After five hundred bullets were fired into James's body, he was dragged up the street. A group of white men, women, and children paraded behind the body.

At first, Ida's husband, Ferdinand, urged black leaders to approach the Illinois governor. He wanted to persuade the governor to enforce a new law that said a sheriff would lose his job if he allowed a prisoner to be taken and lynched. But Ferdinand could not get anyone to agree to see the governor. So he turned to Ida at dinner one night and said that she would have to go. At first Ida refused. Many black men had accused Ida of jumping the gun and rushing to handle matters before they could take care of things themselves. So Ida decided to stay home. But then thirteen-year-old Charles pleaded with her to go. He said that if she didn't go, no one else would. How could she refuse?

Ida took the train to Cairo the next morning to get the facts. She interviewed the black residents of Cairo. She read newspaper accounts of the lynching. She found out that the sheriff had not attempted to protect the accused black man, his prisoner.

Sheriff Davis had a hearing before the governor, where he planned to ask for his job back. On that day, Ida entered the meeting room and discovered she was the only black person there. Ida understood the black residents' fear. Ida knew the black people still had to live in the town once this case was settled. If the sheriff lost his job, angry whites might be likely to attack blacks in the community. But Ida knew that courage was needed to stop lynchings.

Ida gave a wonderful speech. Every one of the white men in the courtroom shook her hand when she was finished. Even the sheriff shook her hand and said he bore no hard feelings toward her. The governor issued a statement saying that Davis could not get his job back as sheriff because he had not properly protected his prisoner. And the governor emphasized that lynching would no longer be tolerated in Illinois.

This changed the way accused prisoners were handled in Illinois. When a sheriff saw signs of trouble with a mob, he would immediately call the governor for troops. Ida never heard of another lynching in that state.

With that settled, Ida turned her attention back to Chicago. She realized that the black men of the city needed a permanent place to gather. Chicago didn't offer the men much. The YMCAs and gymnasiums did not welcome blacks. It seemed that black men were only welcome in saloons, poolrooms, and gambling houses.

Ida was disturbed. She felt that black men would commit fewer crimes if they were involved in worthwhile activities. So she searched for a building where black men could gather. Victor F. Lawson, owner and publisher of the *Daily News,* offered to help. He donated money so that a reading room could be started in an empty building at 2830 State Street.

The facility opened on May 1, 1910, and was known as the Negro Fellowship League Reading Room and Social Center for men and boys. Ida joyfully selected the books for a library at the center. Upstairs she put beds where men could sleep for fifteen cents a night.

The neighborhood was rough. The day the center opened, the howling of drunken men greeted Ida. But Ida was not frightened by their rowdy behavior. She walked among the group of men, asked them to be quiet, then invited them to the center's Sunday meetings. Ida didn't have any trouble with the men. For ten years, Ida's center gave black men a place to read, play checkers, and hunt for a job.

Ida took up another battle when Illinois lawmakers began considering whether to give women the right to vote. Ida had been a member of the Women's Suffrage Association—a voting rights club—as long as she lived in Illinois. But other black club women hadn't seemed interested in this topic.

Ida knew she had to get black women interested in a hurry. She wanted to make sure that if white women got the right to vote, black women did too. So Ida helped organize the Alpha Suffrage Club to work for black women's right to vote. She urged women to join her efforts. She believed that with the vote, black women could help their race.

Black women were discouraged at first. They told Ida that their families pressured them to stay at home. But Ida encouraged them to become active. She advised them to tell their husbands that the women wanted to help put a black man on the city council.

In 1913, when Illinois women—black and white— were allowed to vote in their own city's elections, Ida urged black women to vote. When a group of white Chicago women marched in the city to protest that women should be allowed to vote in all elections, Ida and other black women marched along with the white women. Ida's eight-year-old daughter Alfreda marched with them.

Then the National Women's Suffrage Association planned to march in Washington, D.C., on March 3, 1913. The white leaders of the association told Ida she could not march with them. They were afraid that Ida's presence would anger the Southern white women in the march. But the Illinois women wanted Ida with them. So Ida marched with the other eight thousand women— Illinois white women by her side.

These women lead the women's suffrage parade down Pennsylvania Avenue in Washington, D.C., on March 3, 1913.

10

FAITH, FACTS, AND COURAGE

During World War I, blacks continued to leave the South, hoping to find jobs in Northern steel mills and factories. They hoped there would be less racial prejudice in the North. But Northern white workers didn't like the idea of blacks taking jobs and moving into their neighborhoods. Race riots erupted in several cities.

In July 1918, a race riot shook East St. Louis, Illinois— a filthy, crowded factory city. The riot lasted for two days. Almost one million dollars of property was destroyed and 150 black citizens were killed.

After Ida read about the riot, she met with the Negro Fellowship League. They decided that Ida should go to East St. Louis to get the facts to present to the Illinois governor. They collected money for her expenses, and she left the next day.

When Ida stepped off the train at the East St. Louis stop, the engineer of the train yelled at her to get back on the train. Going into the city was dangerous. But the warnings didn't stop Ida. She needed to collect facts to take to the governor.

Ida met black women who were returning to their homes. She traveled with these women in a Red Cross truck guarded by two soldiers. Many of the women found their homes looted. Pianos, furniture, and bedding had been destroyed. Windows had been broken. Some houses had been burned.

When Ida returned to Chicago with her report for the governor, she discovered that several leading citizens had already gone to the governor. They told him that Ida was a radical and not to pay attention to her.

Ida told this news to the congregation at the Bethel A.M.E. Church. Hearing of this, the congregation organized a group to go to the governor with Ida's report. Ida went with them and told the governor that during the riot, soldiers had stood by and watched black people being attacked. The governor responded that if Ida could get people from East St. Louis to testify about the riots, he would try to do something about it.

Ida went back to East St. Louis. But she had trouble finding anyone who was willing to testify with the facts. Thousands of blacks had left East St. Louis, fleeing the violence there. Others were worried that Ida's group was going to stir up more trouble. Ida found out that blacks involved in the riot were receiving long prison sentences, while white rioters were getting shorter sentences. Dr.

Six blocks of buildings—most of them black-owned houses—burned to the ground in East St. Louis during the race riots in 1918.

Bundy, a black dentist, was sentenced to life imprisonment for leading a group to get guns with which to defend themselves during the riot. When she learned of this, Ida returned to Chicago and wrote an article in the *Defender*. She asked readers to raise money to help pay for lawyers to defend Dr. Bundy. Her article was a success. People from around the country sent money, and Dr. Bundy was freed.

By 1918 the Barnetts moved to a large house on Chicago's Grand Boulevard. The house had previously been owned by a wealthy white family. It had parquet floors and marble sinks. But white neighbors did not welcome prosperous professional blacks like the Barnetts. Whites took the attitude that the blacks were "invading." When Ida and Ferdinand moved to Grand Boulevard, they heard of whites hurling bombs into black houses. In little over a year, twenty-five houses belonging to black people or to realtors who sold to blacks were bombed. In May 1919, the front porch of a house on Grand Boulevard was blown up, and its windows were shattered.

Ida knew that things would only get worse. She wrote a letter to the *Chicago Tribune* asking city officials to do something before there was a riot in the city. But they did nothing. Tension between whites and blacks grew as people quarreled over housing, jobs, education, and recreational spots.

Then one July day in 1919, a black teenager swam into a white swimming area at a Chicago beach. Whites stoned him, and he drowned. A full-scale race riot broke out. For five days, white gangs attacked lone blacks. Black gangs attacked white storekeepers in black neighborhoods.

In Ida's city, whites sped around in cars shooting at blacks. Blacks shot back. During this violent spree, over five hundred people were injured. Mobs and lone gunmen murdered sixteen blacks and fifteen whites. Police officers killed seven blacks. One thousand people were left homeless.

While most people, including Ida's husband and children, stayed behind locked doors, Ida walked the streets collecting facts. Ida was concerned that only blacks were being accused of rioting, and she didn't want Attorney General Brundage to handle the investigation. Brundage had handled the investigation of the East St. Louis riot. As a result, fifteen black men had been sentenced to long prison sentences for defending themselves against whites.

In the fall of that year, violence erupted in Elaine, Arkansas. Trouble started when black sharecroppers refused to sell their cotton for less than they could afford. Angered by this, whites accused blacks of plotting to kill whites in the area. When black farmers held a meeting in a church to form a union, the town's sheriff went into the church, shooting. In the end, about two hundred blacks

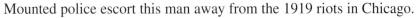

Mounted police escort this man away from the 1919 riots in Chicago.

Police put a dead black man in a police van during the 1919 race riots in Chicago.

and forty whites were killed. Twelve blacks were sentenced to death in the electric chair.

When Ida heard this, she headed a committee to write letters of protest to the president of the United States and to the governor of Arkansas. The letter sent to the governor said that if the twelve black men were electrocuted, there would be a movement to encourage blacks to leave Arkansas. Since Arkansas needed black labor, the governor could not ignore the letter. He called a group of white and black people together to discuss the matter. The group told him they thought the twelve men had not received a fair trial. So the governor canceled the electrocution and ordered a new trial.

As a result of a letter Ida printed in the *Chicago Defender*, people from all over the country began sending money to pay for the men's defense. Then in January 1922, Ida went to Little Rock, Arkansas, to the jail where the twelve men had been transferred. Ida was putting her life in danger by doing this. Even though she had left Memphis thirty years earlier, she was still considered a serious troublemaker in the South and could have been attacked by white mobs.

Ida went to the jail hidden among a group of women—wives and mothers of the twelve men—so the prison guards did not see her. When the group of women got to the jail bars, the leader of the group whispered to the men. She told them that Mrs. Barnett was here to see them.

The men's faces brightened with hope. They told her that they had been beaten and given electric shocks and that a mob had tried to break into the jail to lynch them. Officials had tried to force the black men into saying that they had plans to kill whites and take their property. But the black men had never planned to do this.

Then the men sang for Ida. They sang about dying and forgiving their enemies. Ida went up to the bars. She told the men to stop singing about dying. She told them to pray to live and believe that God would set them free.

Ida returned to Chicago and wrote a pamphlet about the Arkansas riot. A year later, she found out that the men had been freed.

AFTERWORD

In her later years, Ida continued to remain active in community and political events. In 1930 she ran for the office of Illinois state senator, though she lost the election.

During the last three years of her life, she wrote her autobiography. She wanted to be sure that the facts of her life's work were accurately recorded. She hoped that some day black youth would be inspired by her words to continue the fight for equal justice. Ida B. Wells-Barnett died on March 25, 1931, of kidney failure.

Though many Americans may not be familiar with Ida B. Wells-Barnett and her accomplishments, she has not been forgotten. History books now often mention her name when speaking of the great black leaders of her era. In Chicago, the Barnetts' beautiful home at 3624 Grand Boulevard—now Martin Luther King Boulevard—is a national historical landmark. And in 1990, the U.S. Postal Service issued a stamp in commemoration of Ida B. Wells.

Many words have been used to describe Ida. Some saw her as "elegant" and "regal." Some admired her courage and honesty. Others labeled her as a stubborn troublemaker. In 1885, Ida wrote an article for the *New York Freeman* entitled "Woman's Mission." In the article, Ida asked the question, "What is, or should be, woman?"

A woman is "not merely a bundle of flesh and bones," she wrote. A woman should be more than something to dress up and look pretty, she thought. A woman should be "a strong, bright presence . . . with a sense of her mission on earth and a desire to fill it."

Ida B. Wells wrote these challenging words when she was twenty-three. She lived by these words for the rest of her life. She did not ask more of others than she asked of herself. She knew that she and others could make a difference in the country if they let their voices be heard. Ida believed her mission on earth was to save her people from lynching mobs and to lead her people to the gate of full freedom and justice.

Ida B. Wells-Barnett was a strong, bright presence.

NOTES

Page 10
After the Civil War, Elizabeth Wells wrote letters to people in Virginia, trying to find the rest of her family. But she never found them.

Page 14
Shaw University was later named Rust University. When Ida attended school there, the instruction included the early grades through college-level courses.

Page 18
The term "Reconstruction" usually refers to the period after the Civil War to 1877, when there was a reorganization of the South.

Page 18
In 1873, when Ida was eleven, Alexander K. Davis was elected Mississippi's lieutenant governor, and Thomas W. Cardozo was elected state superintendent of education. In 1874, a friend of her father's and a former slave, James Hill, became Mississippi's secretary of state.

Page 22
The Howard Association was an organization that cared for the sick.

Page 26
There were no Jim Crow laws yet. Jim Crow laws were passed to keep blacks apart from whites. These laws separated the races in such things as railroad cars, restaurants, theaters, streetcars, parks, and playgrounds.

Page 27
Ida's diary became an important historical document. It is one of the few personal accounts of black life in Memphis during the 1880s.

Page 47
For statistics, Ida relied on the information published by the *Chicago Tribune.*

Page 50
As slaves, black people were never addressed as Mr., Mrs., or Miss. So when slavery ended, black people (including Ida and her friends) enjoyed and made a point of calling each other Mr. and Miss instead of using their first names.

Page 61
Ida was the first black American to be hired as a correspondent for the *Chicago Inter-Ocean.*

Page 61
Members of the London Anti-Lynching Committee included the Duke of Argyll, son-in-law of Queen Victoria, and A. E. Fletcher, editor of the *London Daily Chronicle.*

Page 91
Sharecroppers were farmers who rented land from a landlord and worked the land for a share of the crop and the income. The Elaine, Arkansas, sharecroppers wanted to join together (form a union) and as a group demand that they get a fair price for their cotton.

BIBLIOGRAPHY

Books and Articles by Ida B. Wells

Crusade for Justice: The Autobiography of Ida B. Wells. Edited by Alfreda M. Duster. Chicago: University of Chicago Press, 1970.

The Memphis Diary of Ida B. Wells. Edited by Miriam DeCosta-Willis. Boston: Beacon Press, 1995.

On Lynchings (Southern Horrors, A Red Record, Mob Rule in New Orleans). Salem, New Hampshire: Ayer Company, 1993.

Books and Articles about Ida B. Wells

Banks, William M. *Black Intellectuals: Race and Responsibility in American Life.* New York: Norton, 1996.

DeCosta-Willis, Miriam. "Ida B. Wells's Diary: A Narrative of the Black Community of Memphis in the 1880s." *The West Tennessee Historical Society Papers* 45 (December 1991): 35–47.

Freedman, Suzanne. *Ida B. Wells-Barnett and the Antilynching Crusade.* Brookfield, Connecticut: Millbrook Press, 1994.

Giddings, Paula. "Woman Warrior—Ida B. Wells, Crusader-Journalist." *Essence* (February 1988): 75, 76, 142, 146.

Haynes, Richard M. *Ida B. Wells: Antilynching Crusader.* Austin, Texas: Raintree Steck-Vaughn, 1994.

Lerner, Gerda, ed. *Black Women in White America: A Documentary History.* New York: Vintage Books, 1972.

Lerner, Gerda. "Community Work of Black Club Women." *Journal of Negro History* 59 (April 1974): 158–167.

McMurry, Linda O. *To Keep the Waters Troubled: The Life of Ida B. Wells.* New York: Oxford University Press, 1998.

Sterling, Dorothy. *Black Foremothers: Three Lives.* Old Westbury, New York: The Feminist Press, 1979.

Sterling, Dorothy, ed. *We Are Your Sisters (Black Women in the Nineteenth Century)*. New York: Norton, 1984.

Thompson, Mildred I. *Ida B. Wells-Barnett: An Exploratory Study of an American Black Woman, 1893–1930*. Brooklyn: Carlson Publishing, 1990.

Townes, Emilie M. "Ida B. Wells-Barnett: An Afro-American Prophet." *The Christian Century* (March 15, 1989): 285–286.

Trimiew, Darryl M. *Voices of the Silenced: The Responsible Self in a Marginalized Community*. Cleveland: The Pilgrim Press, 1993.

Truman, Margaret. *Women of Courage*. New York: William Morrow, 1976.

Tucker, David M. "Miss Ida B. Wells and Memphis Lynching." *Phylon* 32, 2 (summer 1971): 112–122.

Other Sources

Foner, Eric. *Reconstruction: America's Unfinished Revolution, 1863–1877*. New York: Harper & Row, 1988.

Henri, Florette. *Black Migration: Movement North, 1900–1920*. Garden City, New York: Anchor Press/Doubleday, 1975.

Hughes, Langston, and Milton Meltzer. *A Pictorial History of the Negro in America*. New York: Crown Publishers, 1968.

Loewen, James W., and Charles Sallis, eds. *Mississippi: Conflict and Change*. New York: Pantheon, 1980.

McFeely, William S. *Frederick Douglass*. New York: Norton, 1991.

Meltzer, Milton, ed. *The Black Americans: A History in Their Own Words, 1619–1983*. New York: Thomas Y. Crowell, 1984.

Meltzer, Milton. *The Truth about the Ku Klux Klan*. New York: Franklin Watts, 1982.

Rudwick, Elliott M., and August Meier. "Black Man in the 'White City': Negroes and the Colombian Exposition, 1893." *Phylon* 26 (Winter 1965): 354–361.

Severn, Bill. *The Right to Vote*. New York: Ives Washburn, 1972.

Tolnay, Stewart E., and E. M. Beck. *A Festival of Violence: An Analysis of Southern Lynchings, 1882–1930.* Chicago: University of Illinois Press, 1995.

Tuttle, William M. Jr. "Contested Neighborhoods and Racial Violence: Prelude to the Chicago Riot of 1919." *Journal of Negro History* 55 (October 1970): 266–288.

___. "Views of a Negro during 'the Red Summer' of 1919." *Journal of Negro History* 61 (July 1966): 209–218.

Videorecording

Ida B. Wells: A Passion for Justice. New York: William Greaves Productions, 1989. Videorecording.

INDEX